"There are two things
no man will admit he can't do well:
drive and make love."

***Stirling Moss***

*First published in Great Britain in 1997 by*
*Chameleon Books*
*106 Great Russell Street*
*London WC1B 3LJ*



*CIP data for this title is available from the British Library*

*ISBN 0233 99 180 8*

*Book and jacket design by Generation Studio*

*Printed by Graficas Zamudio Printek, S.A.L. in Spain*

*André Deutsch Ltd is a subsidiary of VCI plc.*

*ACKNOWLEDGEMENTS:*

*Special thanks to Ted Macauley, Paul Sudbury, Mark Peacock, Mary Killingworth, Catherine McNeill, Phil McNeill, Joanne Meeks all at Generation Associates, all keen motor racing fans across the country and the man who made it all possible – Tim Forrester.*

*A special thanks to Adrian Murrell and all the lads at Allsport.*

*PHOTOGRAPH ACKNOWLEDGEMENTS*
*ALLSPORT*
*COVER PICTURE : PASCAL RONDEAU*

*PASCAL RONDEAU. PAGES : 14 16/17 19 20 24/25 27 32/33 40-44 46/47 48/49 54/55 59-66 74/75 88/89 92-94 96/97 106*
*MICHEAL COOPER. PAGES : 11 35 68/69 83 95 99*
*JEAN-MARC LOUBAT. PAGES : 13 15 102/103*
*MIKE HEWITT. PAGES : 34 38 50/51 72/73*
*VINCENT KALUT. PAGES : 8 56/57 100/101*
*BEN RADFORD. PAGES : 6/7 22 98*
*JOHN GICHIGI. PAGES : 30 36/37 110*
*ANTON WANT. PAGES : 70/71 80/81 86*
*ALAIN PATRICE. PAGES : 45 84/85*
*CHRIS COLE. PAGE : 10*
*STEVE MUNDAY. PAGE : 26*
*MARK THOMPSON. PAGE : 52*
*HOWARD BOYLAN. PAGE : 53*
*EMMANUEL ZURINI. PAGES : 78/79*
*CLIVE MASON. PAGE : 87*
*AGINCI VANDYSTADT. PAGES : 90/91*

*Dedicated to*
*George and Betty Crowe*

Grand Prix fanatics and those insatiable collectors, like me, of Formula One facts and figures and offbeat snippets of information and trivia will enjoy this unique little effort.

And who says there's no fun in Formula One? There are a good few laughs and lighthearted moments, some of them featuring my prophecies that went immediately wrong on air.

It's a great sport to be involved in from the inside and I, for one, a passionate follower, love to learn as much as I can about it.

I hope this book helps you enjoy you racing just that little bit more.

*Murray Walker*

GAULOISES

***"Christ, I must never eat a Vindaloo again!"***

Ayrton Senna, after a bad-tempered scuffle with Mansell in the pits at the Belgian Grand Prix: "When a man holds you round the throat, I do not think he has come to apologise."

When Damon Hill, promoted from the ranks of test driver to a frontline driver for Williams, was asked how he would cope with Senna as his new teammate, he brought Star Trek Spock into play. "What's Ayrton going to do? Fix me with a Vulcan mind grip or something?"

Irishman Eddie Irvine, recruited from Japan to join Eddie Jordan's F1 team: "What a start to my Grand Prix career. I get punched by Senna in my first face, crash in my second, destroy four cars in my third and get banned from my fourth. People are going to think I'm some kind of nutter."

Ferrari's impish Ulsterman Eddie Irvine's mischief knew no bounds – and ex-BBC, now ITV, pit lane reporter Tony Jardine can vouch for that. He pounced on Irvine after yet another Ferrari breakdown in the 1996 campaign and held an eye-to-eye intensive live interview with the then not-so-fast Eddie. And all credit to Jardine's professionalism, as he miraculously managed to keep his face straight and his questions still rolling as, out of sight of the camera, Irvine emptied a litre of icy water down the unruffled Beeb broadcaster's trousers.

Diet is a big thing in sport in more ways than one. In Japan, F1 drivers were impressed by the average Sumo wrestler, who weighs in at around 260 kilograms and fattens up an 18,500 calories a day. He gorges two fried flounders, 12 dumplings, 500 grams of grilled beef, close on a bucketful of stew with endless bowls of rice, two big fried chicken legs and a mass of butter biscuits, all washed down with two litres of beer and two big glasses of saki.

A slim-line racer, existing on 2,000 calories a day, sips a bowl of vegetable soup and nibbles one slice of wholemeal bread, no butter, with a small plate of pasta and steamed veg. He has a treat of dried fruit and nuts, and fruit juice or mineral water to swill it down – and it keeps his weight steady at around 65 kilograms.

So how *does* Schumacher spend his £20 million a year?

***"How come you can't find a sponsor for below the waist?"***

*Michael Schumacher*
*is not a smug*
*bastard ... Official.*

*"What do you mean too out-of-touch for a comeback?"*

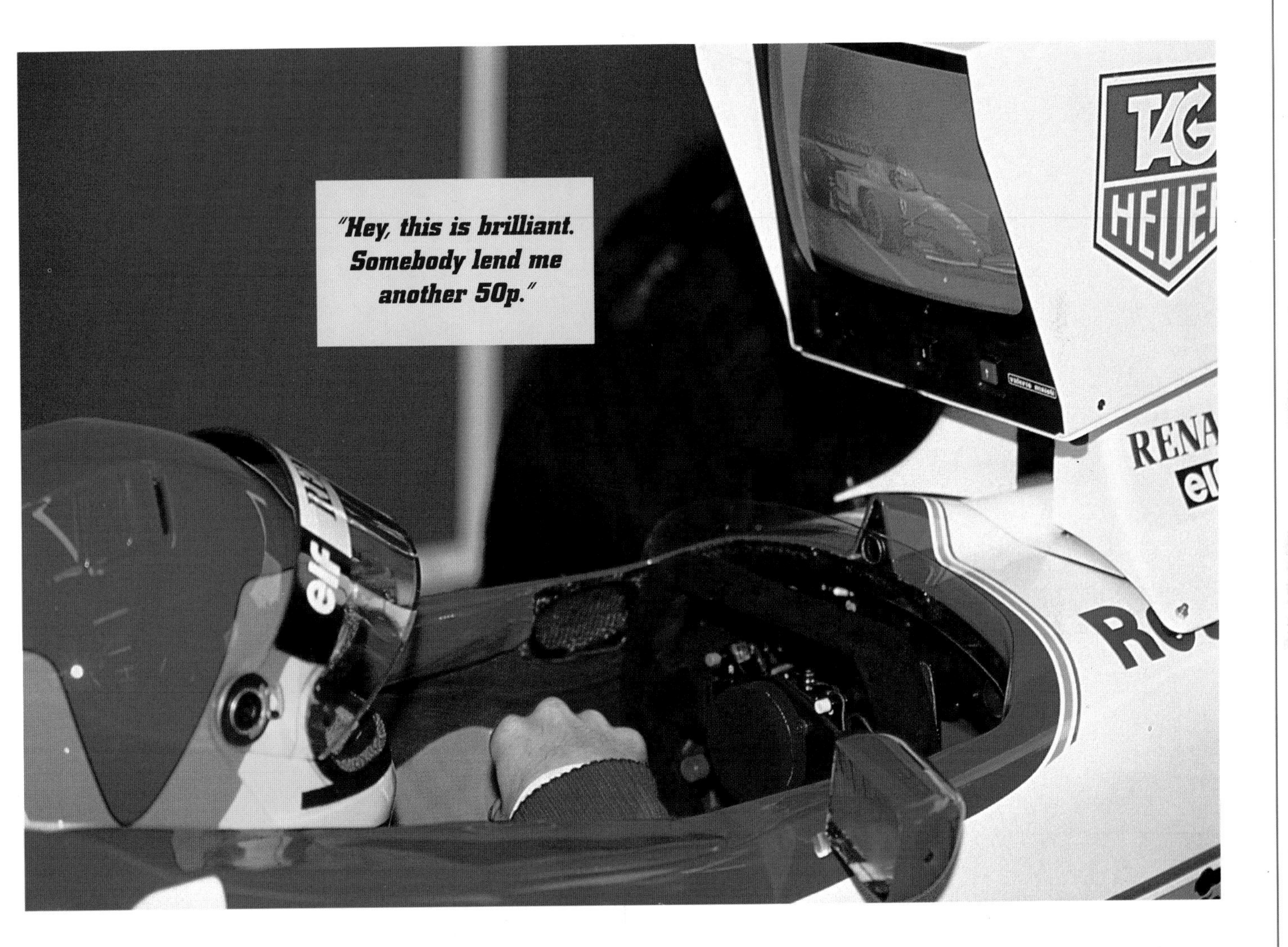


***"Hey, this is brilliant. Somebody lend me another 50p."***

*"Zat's one in ze eye for der Englander, fnar, fnar."*

***Jacques Villeneuve remembers he forgot to go before putting his suit on.***

"You win some, you lose some,
you wreck some."
– Dale Earnhardt
EAGLE

Marlboro
Marlboro

Talk about amazing ... Tonino Ascari, the 1964 Italian Formula 3 title holder, never followed the famous family tradition of competing in F1. No wonder. His father Alberto and his grandad Antonio had both been Grand Prix winners – and both were killed racing. Antonio died in an Alfa Romeo carrying the race number eight when he was 36 on July 26. Alberto, who was ferociously superstitious, forever hated the number eight and refused to race on the 26th of the month ... or without wearing his lucky blue helmet.

However, in 1955, after twice winning the world championship, he somehow survived when his car nosedived into the harbour at Monaco. Four days later, aching and bruised from the spectacular crash, he drove to Monza in Italy to watch Euginio Castellotti test a Ferrari sports car. He certainly had no intention of driving that day but almost as an afterthought he jumped into the car... the old racing drivers' urge to get behind the wheel as soon as possible after an accident. Nobody knows why, but the car somersaulted and Alberto was killed. It was May 26 ...

His lifespan was just three days longer than his father's. Alberto had always stressed that his offspring never saw him race and he kept them at a distance. "I don't want them to get too fond of me," he said. "One of these days I may never come back."

The OLDEST driver to start a Grand Prix was Frenchman Louis Chiron. He was 55 years and 292 days old when he roared off the line in Monaco in 1965.

The YOUNGEST driver ever to start in a Grand Prix was New Zealander Mike Thackwell. He was 19 years and 182 days old at the Canadian Grand Prix in 1980. But an accident at the start forced a re-run and he had to surrender his car to his more senior Tyrell teammate Jean-Pierre Jarier ... so he didn't actually race.

The legendary Argentinian Juan-Manuel Fangio's Grand Prix strike rate was a phenomenal 24 victories from only 51 races and he started from the front row of the grid an amazing 48 times. His titles were won in four different makes – Alfa Romeo, Mercedes, Ferrari and Maserati.

The YOUNGEST winner was New Zealand's Bruce McLaren, who was 22 years and 104 days of age when he sped to victory in the 1959 United States Grand Prix at Sebring.

The OLDEST Grand Prix victor was Italian Luigi Gagioli, who was 53 when he clinched first place in the French Grand Prix.

Damon Hill openly acknowledges Nigel Mansell's remarkable dullness

***I have never heard Damon Hill say an unkind word about anybody…***

***but thoughts … thoughts are different …***

***very, very different...***

Formula One ringmaster Bernie Ecclestone headed the list of racing's richest with a Sunday newspaper wealth listing of £275 million. Williams team owner Frank Williams was valued at £50 million, McLaren boss Ron Dennis at £45 million, and The richest driver in Britain was the former world champion Nigel Mansell, now retired, who has reputedly banked £35 million.

Alberto Ascari, who was killed in mysterious circumstances in a crash at Monza in 1955 while unofficially testing a Ferrari sports car, achieved the greatest number of consecutive victories. But the record was split across two seasons. He won nine times on the run between 1952 and the Belgian Grand Prix in 1953.

1997 – Williams' driver Jacques Villeneuve triumphed over second-placed Eddie Irvine in a Ferrari.

Nigel Mansell grabbed NINE wins in his 1992 championship winning season – and that was equalled by German wonderboy Michael Schumacher in 1995, the year he won his second F1 title.

Stirling Moss won the 100th GP, Jackie Stewart the 200th, Ronnie Peterson the 300th, Niki Lauda 400th and Nelson Piquet the 500th.

The Jordan team celebrated their 100th GP in Argentina – newcomer Ralf Schumacher, Michael's kid brother, shunted his teammate Giancarlo Fisichella off the track to grab third place.

Ron Dennis, the unsmiling boss of McLaren, sympathizing with Irishman Eddie Jordan who had just lost his star find Michael Schumacher to Flavio Briatore's Benetton team: "Welcome to the Piranha Club."

Italian ace Tazio Nuvolari had Grand Prix gamesmanship down to a fine art. One of his unnerving ploy was to suddenly leap up in his seat and yell abuse at the starter to unsettle his rivals on the grid. "I will do anything to win a race," he threatened without shame, "anything, anything, anything. I don't waste time being sporting."

"It was not difficult for me to reject McLaren's offer. I am happy at Benetton. We are building something special here and I want to see it completed." – World Champion Michael Shumacher before Ferrari tempted him with a £20million a year offer

Martin Brundle, who quit Formula One with Jordan to become Murray Walker's sidekick on ITV in 1997, said in his racing days: "To the spectators I am a crash helmet buried inside a car that is flashing past them at 200mph. I am a fleeting glimpse of humanity. I have had more recognition from two appearances on Question of Sport than anything I have ever done in F1."

"The thing that holds us all together is happiness."
– Finnish ace J J Lehto just before he was fired by Benetton

Frank Williams, confined to a wheelchair after being paralysed in a road crash in the South of France, says philosophically: "I took one bend too many too fast. I was an accident waiting to happen." And: "I was a physical leader – I learned to become a mental leader."

Belgian Grand Prix driver Bertrand Gachot was jailed for 18 months for spraying a London cabbie with CS gas in a road rage attack. "It cost me almost £1 million," he said, "so it must be the most expensive accommodation in Europe. It is certainly the least attractive."
– A banner unveiled outside the British Embassy in Brussels proclaimed.

On average each team sends 45 personnel to each Grand Prix. It includes the team principal or owner, chief designer, team manager, team co-ordinator, five engineers, a chief mechanic, nine mechanics (three per car), a fabricator, three gearbox mechanics, two engineering support technicians, six truck drivers (who double as tyre and fuel crewman), two marketing co-ordinators, a press officer, four hospitality staff, a physio, two electronic engineers, two radio engineers. Each driver has his own dedicated race engineer who reports all changes in the set-up to the chief mechanic.

The team manager is in overall control and is involved in deciding tactics in consultation with the team principal, the race engineers and the driver.

The team co-ordinator controls freight and personnel movements and accommodation, and advises on the sporting regulations and generally manages the team's affairs.

A pit crew of 21 are involved in each fuel and tyre stop.

After each Grand Prix the cars are returned to the factory, where they are completely stripped down and each component is assessed for wear and tear. They are then rebuilt, using new parts where necessary, before being transported to the next race. If there is back-to-back racing outside Europe – the "flyaways" – then the cars will be rebuilt at the next track from spares jumbo-jetted into the country.

***Ferrari are widely recognised for putting their drivers through rigorous fitness procedures***

***"I can. I can see straight through."***

In the chaos that enveloped Nigel Mansell after his nation-stirring win at the 1992 British Grand Prix at Silverstone, fan Ian Neild, who should not have been on the track anyway, tripped and fell under his hero's Williams as it headed through the mass back to the *parc fermé*.

An anxious Mansell, lost in all the jubilation, had to grin as the bruised and battered Neild climbed back to his feet and yelled: "I'm all right – can I have your helmet?"

Later, Neild told Mansell: "The accident didn't hurt me at all. It's an honour to have been under your wheels. I was more worried about you. I have followed you all over and now I have met you face to face. It really is a dream come true."

Brazilian Rubens Barrichello walked away from a terrifying 170 mph crash during qualifying for the San Marino Grand Prix at the fearsome Imola circuit, where his buddy Ayrton Senna died. As he was being loaded on to a stretcher he said: "I don't know what happened. But I think it was very quick. It is a bit difficult to breathe because my nose and hands hurt a bit. You must excuse me ... I'm off to play with the nurses now."

***"Hey! These are great. I can't hear a word he's saying."***

RENAULT
elf
5
Canon
Canon

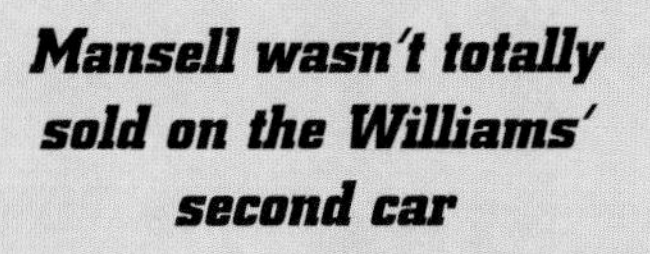

***Mansell wasn't totally sold on the Williams' second car***

*"Unless I am very much mistaken ...*
*I am very much mistaken."* –

***The slogan emblazoned on the Murray Walker Fan Club T-shirts***

*"We are now on the 73rd lap ... and the next one will be the 74th."*

*"I don't make mistakes. I make prophesies that go wrong right away."*

*"Either the car is stationary ... or it's on the move."*

*"Once again Damon Hill is modest in defeat."*

*"You can see the gap between Mansell and Piquet is rather more than just visual."*

*"I imagine that the conditions in those cars today are totally unimaginable."*

*"It's not quite a curve, it's a straight actually."*

*"And now the other boot is on the other Schumacher."*

*"You can't see a digital clock because there isn't one."*

ENERVIT
Ford
TECHNOGYM
MILD SEVEN

*"Right, so you want*
*six Big Macs,*
*eight Quarter Pounders,*
*14 large fries,*
*and a Diet Coke."*

***Nigel Mansell is so brave, but such a moaner. He should have 'He Who Dares, Whines' embroidered on his overalls.'***
***– Simon Barnes, The Times***

***Fastest man on four wheels, five million pounds a year, a cracking girlfriend, and all some smart-arse book publisher can do is point out that you're going bald***

10:00
VAUXHALL
RENAULT

***The toilet arrangements at Silverstone are acknowledged as the worst on the GP circuit***

***The new Benetton overalls Michael Schumacher was invited to get into***

The first woman to drive in Formula One was the dainty and diminutive Maria Theresa de Fillipis. She finished tenth in a Maserati at Spa, Belgium in 1958 – the year Tony Brooks gave Vanwall its only win at the gruelling Ardennes circuit. The Vanwall was the first British car ever to win a world championship when it was raced to glory by Brooks and Stirling Moss in the 1957 British Grand Prix at Aintree, scene of the world's greatest steeplechase, the Grand National.

Modern F1 cars are fitted with four or more micro-computer systems that control engine, fuel, gearbox, clutch, throttle and dashboard displays. Hundreds of messages are produced every second and the data is either stored in the car's "black box" on board or relayed via telemetry direct to the engineers in the pits.

It normally takes a team of 20 designers and engineers between four and six months to design and draw the 4000-plus parts that into the make-up of a Grand Prix car.

The fantastic aerodynamic downforces, perfected in wind-tunnels, exerted by an interplay of wings and undertrays is such that a speed of around 150 mph a Formula One car could theoretically be driven upside down across your ceiling without falling off. A high-tech semi-automatic gearbox allows a Grand Prix driver to change gear in a split second ... less than two hundredths of a second in fact. And that is five times faster than a manual gear change.

Cockpit temperatures frequently rise to more than 50 degrees and drivers, protected by fireproof overalls and underclothing, dehydrate to such a level in a two-hour race that they can lose between two and three kilos in weight.

Formula One cars gobble up about 60 litres of fuel per 100 kilometres. In comparison, family cars use 8-10 litres over the same distance. And motorway stop pump petrol, cleaned and purified, goes in to the 200 mph Grand Prix car.

A Formula One car will rocket from standstill to 100 mph and back again to a dead stop in about six seconds.

"Better a spray in London than a dagger in Heysel."

*"There's a girl outside wants to see you, Michael." "What do think she wants?"*
*"Mmm – hard to tell."*

Juan Fangio: "When one runs the risk of losing a sense of proportion it is time to go home, sleep in the same bed in which one dreamed while still a nobody, and to eat the simple, healthy dishes of one's childhood."

Fangio again: "You must always believe you will become the best ... but you must never believe you have done so."

Scots star David Coulthard, who started his F1 career with Williams and won for them in Portugal, and was then fired and snapped up by Ron Dennis at McLaren, where he won the Australian GP in the 1997 curtain-raiser, says: "You know you have arrived in life when you get your name printed on the side of your cap."

In typically grand style Ron Dennis opines: "Motor racing belongs in England."

Ayrton Senna, the year before he was killed in a mystery crash in the San Marion Grand Prix at Imola: "One side of me says go away from this and look after yourself. The other side says you love it, it's been your life, you get so much out of it and you've got the respect of so many people all over the world, you just can't drop it."

And again: "Somebody said you need two lives, one to make mistakes in, the other to enjoy. Well ... I feel I could do with three or four."

***Rubens Barrichello appears unhappy with new arrangements for disposing of urinary fluids during a three-hour race***

***Michael Schumacher tells Grandstand about his on-track rivalry with Damon Hill***

*"No, Ralf, I am thinking that I have the most endearing smile for the ladies."*

Ecclestone on how he gained his power as F1's supremo: "I've been wheeling and dealing since I was eleven, buying and selling pens, bicycles, what have you. Then I went into motor cycles, cars and property – whatever was about to sell and trade. I suppose the word to describe me would be entrepreneur – but that's not a good word. Used car dealer? Well, that sounds evil – but it does have a nice ring to it. I don't recall what I put on my passport – probably Company Director. That covers a multitude of sins. But I work hard for whatever I've got, seven days a week, all over the world and with a lot of sacrifices in my home life, from when I get up to the time I go to bed. It never stops. I won't retire. I'll die in the job."

All said at the age of 65 ...

Bernie Ecclestone, a failed racer who became the most powerful man in world motor sport:

"People who cheat only cheat themselves."

Bernie again on his fabulous Formula One production:

"We are in show business. Worldwide."

Nigel Mansell, nicknamed Il Leone – the Lion – by the Ferrari-mad fans in Italy:

"Before I leave Ferrari or retire I want to go into a restaurant anywhere in Italy and be allowed to pay for a meal."

*"Blow harder or I won't let you out!"*

***"I hope I can get away before the crowd see me."***

Mike Hawthorn was the first British driver to win the World Championship. The playboy ace, who raced wearing a bow tie, made his reputation with daredevil driving in an under-powered Cooper in 1952 – and won his first GP by outdriving and outwitting the maestro Fangio in a Ferrari at the French Grand Prix in 1953.

Hawthorn, devastated at the death of his teammate and best pal Peter Collins in 1958, retired at the end of the season as the reigning champion. Inside three months he, too, was dead – killed in a mystery road smash near his home.

"Why do you say Schumacher has halitosis?"

On being internationally famous Mansell said: "Like all sportsmen I have become a prisoner of my own sport. It is not that I am antisocial or a hermit, but if I leave my hotel room I know I will not be able to do what I want to do. There's no freedom. It is difficult to have a normal conversation. The world we live in is so unreal. That is why it is so important to come home, plant your feet on the ground, and realise what the real world is all about."

Pop group Pink Floyd drummer Nick Mason, a part-time racer and speed freak: "I'm not particularly worried about meeting Michael Jackson, but I do enjoy it when Stirling Moss is around."

Hollywood superstar Paul Newman was sitting in awe of Nigel Mansell as they dined with golfer Greg Norman in Phoenix, Arizona, at the start of the Brummie's IndyCar career with the Newman/Haas team. "I don't care about any of the honours I have received," said the dreamboat actor, "I just wish I could boast that I had won just one of the races you have, Nigel."

Moss, the greatest driver never to win the world championship, says: “If God had wanted us to walk, he’d have give us pogo-sticks instead of feet. Feet are made to fit car pedals.”

Stirling fan Shelagh Poulter-Marron penned a poem for her idol:

*Good eyes, bald head, quick hands.*
*I have a beautiful friend*
*And I thought the old despair*
*would end in love in the end.*
*But I looked into your eyes one day*
*And saw her image there*
*And have gone weeping away.*

The all-time British racing hero reveals: “My father was very bright when he stopped my mother calling me Hamish. Stirling Moss is a name that sticks. It helped.”

**"Absolutely. Both David and I see ourselves enjoying a long future with Williams."**

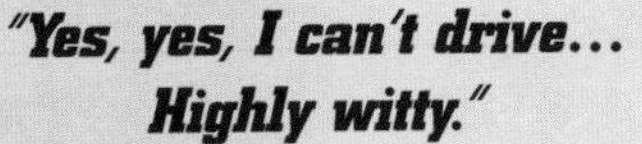


The pit stop, a controversial element in racing because of its inherent dangers during refuelling, was re-introduced to Gerand Prix racing as a clever strategy rather thana necessity by the forward- thinking Brabham team in 1982.
They figured they could turn it into an advantage over their rivals because they would run a big slice of the race on a half tank of petrol and soft tyres and pick up valuable time. A fuel stop with a change of tyres gave them such an advantage than other teams, reluctantly, had to follow suit. However, re-fuelling was banned in 1984.

The idea that the pit stops added to the drama of the race led to the ban being lifted in 1994, and despite misgivings and arguments by the frontline teams, they were re-introduced by the F1A.

*"You may be smiling just now, Nigel, but don't forget, I'm driving you home."*

RENAULT
MILD SEVEN
UNITED COLORS
OF BENETTON.
RENAULT
MILD SEVEN
UNITED COLORS
OF BENETTON.

*"Who's sponsoring us this season then?"*

***"There's a problem. You see the squiggly lines? That's the track. The straight line is the route you took."***

Hunt, who would turn up to official dinners wearing a dinner suit and open-necked shirt and trainers, said: “One day when I retire, my ambition is to go back to being a normal person ... one who likes other people, whom other people like.”

Damon Hill was a punk. He played guitar in a band called Sex Hitler and the Hormones.

Eddie Jordan's best friend is rock star Chris Rea, and he frequently plays drums with the band when they rehearse at Jordan HQ opposite the main gates of Silverstone. The Dubliner organizes the post-race rave-up after the British Grand Prix when his "Jordanairs" band entertain anybody who can find their way into the jam-packed paddock for a barbeque and beer bash among relaxing Formula One superstars.

Prince Michael of Kent, a committed motor race enthusiast and a regular at the British Grand Prix, reveals: "By the time I was 13 I had driven more than 100 difference vehicles up and down our drive."

British Grand Prix winner Johnny Herbert reveals: "I came third in the South of England Scalextric Championships in Leytonstone when I was 13. It was the start of my motor racing career," claims the Essex man.

Damon Hill's dad Graham, Mr Monaco, won the Monte Carlo showpiece race so often – five times, in fact – that Damon thought: "I remember growing up thinking that winning the Monaco Grand Prix was his job."

***"No, the brilliant-looking, sleek, shiny red bit is the Ferrari part. The bit that is smoking is Fiat."***

Grand Prix elder statesman Ken Tyrrell, mentor to Jackie Stewart in his formative Formula One days, recalls the days of racing yore: "Oh what fun! What sport! Hell for leather. No crash hats or flame-proof underpants. Just a silk scarf round your neck, waving to girlfriends and smelling the flowers on the way."

Nigel Mansell, who earned around £10 million a season with Williams in his 1992 championship success, sold his house to fund his racing dreams just after he got married. "When I came into F1 I was very conscious not to upset senior drivers," he claims, "but the general standard of newer drivers is very disturbing."

*"Congratu-bloodly-lations."*

Marlboro
WORLD
Labatt's
GOODYEAR
Labatt's
CAMEL
elf
Labatt's
Marlboro
CHAMPION
sparco
Riccardo Patrese

Professor Syd Wakins, the head of F1's medical panel who attends every race in the championship, says: "I make a lot of jokes about the fact that as a neuro-surgeon I should hardly be required at a motor race because the drivers don't have any brains ... otherwise they wouldn't race."

When Eddie Jordan's team lined up for their 100th Grand Prix in Buenos Aires in April 1997 there were NINE drivers on the Argentine grid who had driven for the talent-spotting Dubliner in Formula One, Formula Three and Formula 3000. They were Giancarlo Fisichella, Ralf Schumacher, world champs Michael Schumacher and Damon Hill, Jean Alesi, Eddie Irvine, Johnny Herbert, Heinz-Harald Frentzen and Rubens Barrichello.

Jacques Villeneuve, poetry in motion, was so badly afflicted by a stomach bug in Buenos Aires that his urgent performance figures of standstill to 100 mph in search of a toilet were the talk of the track. He spent so much time in the press room toilet, the media named the loo after him and ever afterwards, when they were leaving the room, they were going for what was termed "a quick Villeneuve".

Jacques Villeneuve, the youngest ever IndyCar champion at 24, was only the third driver in the history of Grand Prix racing to start from pole position in his debut race when he went to the line in the 1996 Australian round in Melbourne. The other two were Carlos Reutemann and Mario Andretti.

***"Listen old man, can you tell me how to find the girl in the new Benetton overalls."***

RTL
sparco
MILD SEVEN
MAGNETI
TECHNOGYM
elf

"These guys really stink after a race."

GOODYEAR
Rothmans
Rothmans
Rothmans
Rothmans
elf
Damon Hill
elf
MINOL
MILD SEVEN
Bitburger
BENETTON
SPORTSYSTEM

# They wish they hadn't said that...

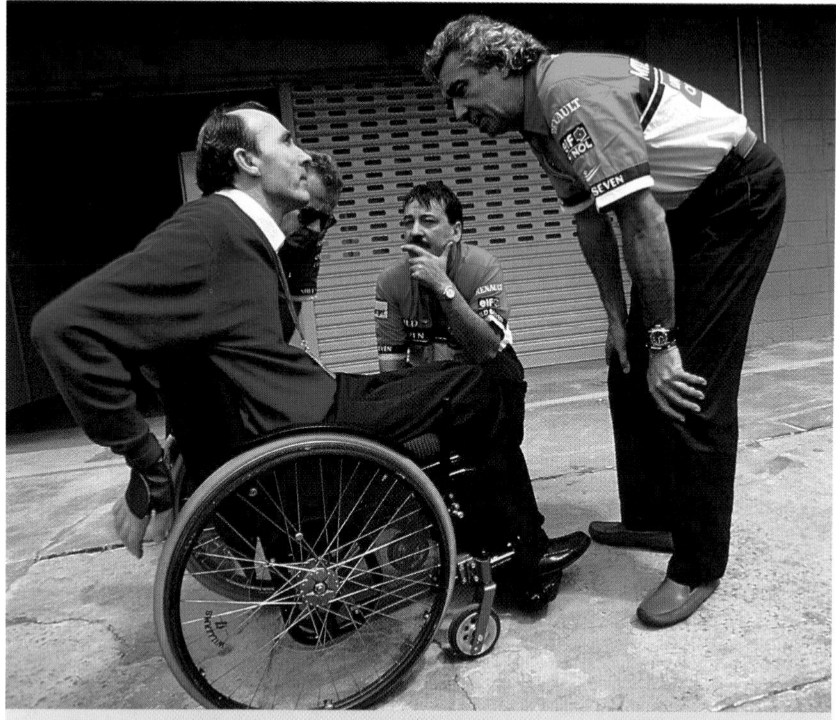


*"Yes, we can put stabilisers on, Frank, but I don't think it'll be safe over 130."*

BBC TV pundit James Hunt: "Your luck goes up and down like swings and roundabouts."

Three-times world champion Jackie Stewart: "I think the Europeans have had this attitude that no one can impregnate their superiority."

"I wouldn't like to be sitting in Prost's shoes right now." – Barry Sheene, ex-world motor cycle champ and Australian Channel 9 commentator.

Lola team boss Eric Broadley only two weeks before his financially strapped Grand Prix outfit pulled out of racing after competing only in the opener in Australia in 1997: "I hope that by the end of four years we will be ready to win the championship." Oops!

"If you qualify in the top six I'll give you a brand new Daytona watch." – Team boss Jackie Stewart to Rubens Barrichello in Argentina in 1997. Barrichello made it into fifth place ... and threw his old wrist watch out of the car as he roared into pit lane.

It was at Melbourne in 1996 that Damon Hill equalled his famous father Graham's record of 14 GP victories. He also equalled the feat of Michael Schumacher, Aussie world champion Alan Jones and Stirling Moss of winning back-to-back races in the same country.

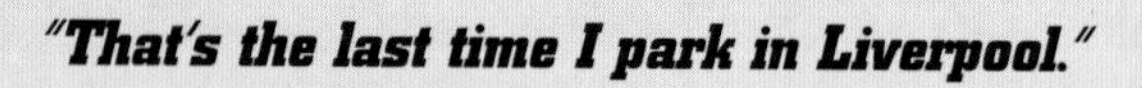

*"That's the last time I park in Liverpool."*

SEGA

***The Benetton crew when they heard that Schumacher was going to Ferrari.***

James Hunt, whose bizarre lifestyle of drugs and drink amazed the world of Grand Prix racing, cared little for what people thought of his antics but did have moments of philosophising wisdom. Like: “Image-making is a risk. I have questioned myself about it and I have tried to be an ostrich and ignore other people’s glamorous and distorted view of me as much as I can. Limelight’s a danger and so is wealth. It’s like giving a dog a big juicy bone. When he didn’t have one he could live without it but once he’s tasted one he hangs on like grim death.”

Team owner Ken Tyrrell's son, Ken Junior, piloted the British Airways 747 jumbo jet loaded with F1 personnel back from Buenos Aires after the 1966 Argentine Grand Prix.

In the 47-year history of GP racing, the winner of the first round has on 21 occasions gone on to win the Formula One title.

The first victims of the rule that stipulates cars have to qualify within 107 per cent of the pole position time were the Italian Ford-Forti team at the 1996 Argentine GP – and that meant a long flight without a race for failures Luca Badoer and Andrea Montermini.

*Schumacher passes the rigorous urine test at the Nurburgring.*

Two drivers in the 1916 Prest-O-Lite Maxwell team at Indianapolis were the first to wear crash helmets. Eddie Rickenbacker and Pete Henderson fashioned them from padded metal hats.

American IndyCar legend Mario Andretti clinched the Formula One title in 1978 and had a record of 12 wins in 128 Grand Prix starts before he quit and returned to America and became, at 53, the oldest winner of an IndyCar event by taking the garland at Phoenix, Arizona 1993.

Veteran Gerhard Berger argued: "if aeroplanes can re-fuel safely at 30,000 feet why , with all our technology, can`t we do it on the ground in complete safety? "

A couple of weeks after Berger`s remark Dutchman Jos Verstappen was trapped in a fireball in the Benetton pit at Hockenhein and was lucky to escape with only a few scorch marks. The blaze was caused by a faulty valve and a junior mechanic was blamed.

*"You will never guess what I have under here."*

14

***"And people try to tell you that motor racing isn't dangerous these days..."***

Diavia
AIR CONDITIONERS
INTERNATIONAL FREIGHT

**Sometimes you can sum up a driver's mood in a single word - and that word is not appearing in this book before the nine o'clock watershed.**

Enzo Ferrari, the tyrant boss of the world-famous Italian marque, argued that any Grand Prix driver who was married with children penalized himself by about one second a lap.

Safety cars were introduced into Grand Prix racing in 1992 as the alternative to stopping a race after a serious incident when the track is blocked by an abandoned car if there is debris that needs to be cleared. The field circulates behind the pace car ... and it annoys the hell out of them because it usually does not travel fast enough and their tyres cool down to dangerous levels – way below the ideal working temperature.

VAUXHALL
CAVALIER
Auto Trader
4
Mobil
MICHELIN

***As sponsors drifted away, Damon Hill became increasingly desperate...***

The Rothmans-Williams team was fined £4.2 million when the French anti-smoking lobby successfully complained about the car carrying a cigarette advertising logo that was seen on national television. But somehow, the fine, set in their world championship-winning year, was never paid because the punishment, mysteriously, was never enforced. Ironically, a year later, the French team Larrousse managed to secure a £3.5 million grant as compensation for lost revenue from banned cigarette sponsorship resulting from the anti-tobacco ruling.

Benetton ran a car with all four-wheel steering towards the end of the 1993 season – but with little movement on the rear wheels.

Brooklands Motor Course, near Weybridge in Surrey, was the world's first purpose-built race circuit in 1907. It was set up by Hugh Locke-King on his estate and had a lap distance of three and three-quarter miles with two long, banked curves. The fastest lap was set by John Cobb in a Napier-Railton in 1935 at an incredible 151.97mph. The last Brooklands meeting was in 1939 and the clubhouse complex now houses a fine motor sport museum.

*"This is what you get for allowing a 12-second pit stop, you clumsy dolt."*

The first woman to race a car was a Madame Laumaille, who drove a De Dion in the 1898 Marseilles to Nice event. She finished fourth – and beat her husband.

The smallest Grand Prix field ever lined up – if that's the right expression – was at the French race staged at the Miramas Autodrome, near Marseilles, in 1926. Just three Bugattis took part. One completed the full distance, the second managed 85 of the 100 laps and the third retired. It was the first round of a brand new Formula and no other team had a car ready in time to race.

The organisers dropped a big clanger: they forgot to include a clause allowing for cancellation if a specified number of entrants failed to appear.

***"A 4.3-second pit stop. Brilliant! Or did we forget something?"***

The first American victory in a major European race went to Jimmy Murphy in the 1921 French Grand Prix at Le Mans. He was driving a Duesenberg, the first GP car to have hydraulic brakes – front wheels only – and he clinched the 322-mile race at an average of 78.10 mph.

**"Goodbye then, it's been great having you in the team an' that, but can you hurry up a bit now, Damon – Frank wants the car back for the new lad."**

Riding mechanics, those brave souls who sat alongside even the most crackpot drivers in hell-for-leather races and frequently fell out of the car or were badly injured when it tipped over, were finally, and no doubt relieved to be, banned from Grand Prix events in 1925.

***Williams were worried if their new car would pass the IFA regulations***

MILD
SEVEN
Flymo
Flymo

***"And then just when Damon's gonna overtake you on the outside – BAM! You ram him off the track."***

NZi
E.CASTRO

Only one man has ever driven in his very first race in the premier event of the year and won … it was Christian Lautenschlager, in a Mercedes, in the 1908 French Grand Prix.

In the same race the first ever fatal Grand Prix accident happened. Driver Cissac and his riding mechanic Schaube were both killed when their Panhard crashed.

The racing term "Pit" found its origins at that race, too. A trench with a counter just above road level that was provided for the team crews was known as the pits – and the term for the working area for mechanics has stuck down the years.

RHÔNE-POULENC
CAMEL
CAMEL
Canon
FIAT
Agip

***And this was just the warm-up lap!***

***Sometimes Mansell's desire for a good start at IndyCar was a bit over-the-top***

Brabham, the once-mighty team named after Sir Jack, the Aussie world champion, collapsed in 1992 – a victim of financial starvation. Its 39th and final Grand Prix was the Hungarian in Budapest, when Damon Hill was driving for them and finding his way as a nearly-broke rookie in Formula One. He finished 11th ... and last.

***"No, Damon, I'm not listening."***
***(PS: Thanks for covering up my bald spot.)***

*"Well, one of us is wrong."*

Shell
parmalat
Kibon
9

"Zer is shit on zur track."

"STOP!!!!!!!!!!!!"

Ahh, they look really tired

***Coulthard's Tips:***
***Don't drink and drive.***
***Try and avoid the M25 if at all possible.***
***Only have 1 girlfriend at a time.***

***"Oh, shit!!!!!!!!!!"***

*"An just when he think's he's got no traction, we all let go."*

Frank Williams on re-signing Nigel Mansell for a three-race comeback to F1 after his sabbatical in IndyCar at racing in America:"I've got too much money and I just had to get rid of it."

Williams again on Mansell: "Brilliant in the car – but a pain in the backside out of it."

The Benetton boss, flamboyant Italian Flavio Briatore, the mastermind behind Michael Schumacher's two world championships, once said: "When I first came into formula One I thought Ron Dennis was a God.

Then, when we went ahead of his team for most of the season, I realised he was just another human being."

"How do you make small fortune from Grand Prix racing? Start with a large one..."

– ***ANON***

"I have tried to hide the fact that I had a title. But I've never come up against this Earl thing within the sport. Everyone accepts me for what I am ... a racing driver ... and that is gratifying." – Johnny Dumfries, the Earl of Dumfries and now the Marquess of Bute, one of the wealthiest men in Britain

When he was performing his laid-back broadcasts on Grand Prix for BBC TV, James would often pop out of the commentary box for a quick joint and fellow airwaves man Murray Walker would cover up: "James has just nipped out to have a look at the far side of the circuit."

Ceasar's Palace, that Las Vegas monument to bad taste and ludicrous hype, staged two Formula One rounds - in 1981 when Aussie Alan Jones won in the William's and 1982 when Michele Alboreto was victorious with a rare Tyrrel triumph.

After the event was scrapped - but when F1 ringmaster Bernie Ecclestone was invited to re-open negotiations for a United States Grand Prix in 1997 his dealings were dogged by drama...a pet Alsatian bit his nose.

Afterwards a notice appeared a notice appeared on the doorway to his ritzy paddock motor home: "Never mind the dog, beware of the owner."

Nigel Mansell, the only driver to hold both the F1 World title and IndyCar championship at the same time before he retired to run a golf and leisure club in Exeter, stresses: "Nobody gave me anything for free. Whatever I have achieved has been through determination, single-mindedness and a dogged will to win."

Innes Ireland, the classic Biggles of a driver, devil-may-care, party-going and charming off the track and coolly ruthless on it, said: "I was lucky. I was 26 when I started racing seriously. I had lost, you see old boy, all the wildness and exuberance of youth. Those things don't help at all. It is very much better to drive with common sense. One needs to be very, very calm."

Ferrari became the first team in Formula One history to score a centry of championship wins when Frenchman Alain Prost, four times the driver's champ, clinched victory in the French Grand Prix in 1990.

Ferrari broke the the all-time record for drivers' wages when they lured World Champion Michael Schumacher from Italian rival team Benetton in 1996 and paid him £20 million a year.

***The air of expectancy is there for all to see as fans queue to kiss Damon Hill's helmet***

# Murray Walker – again

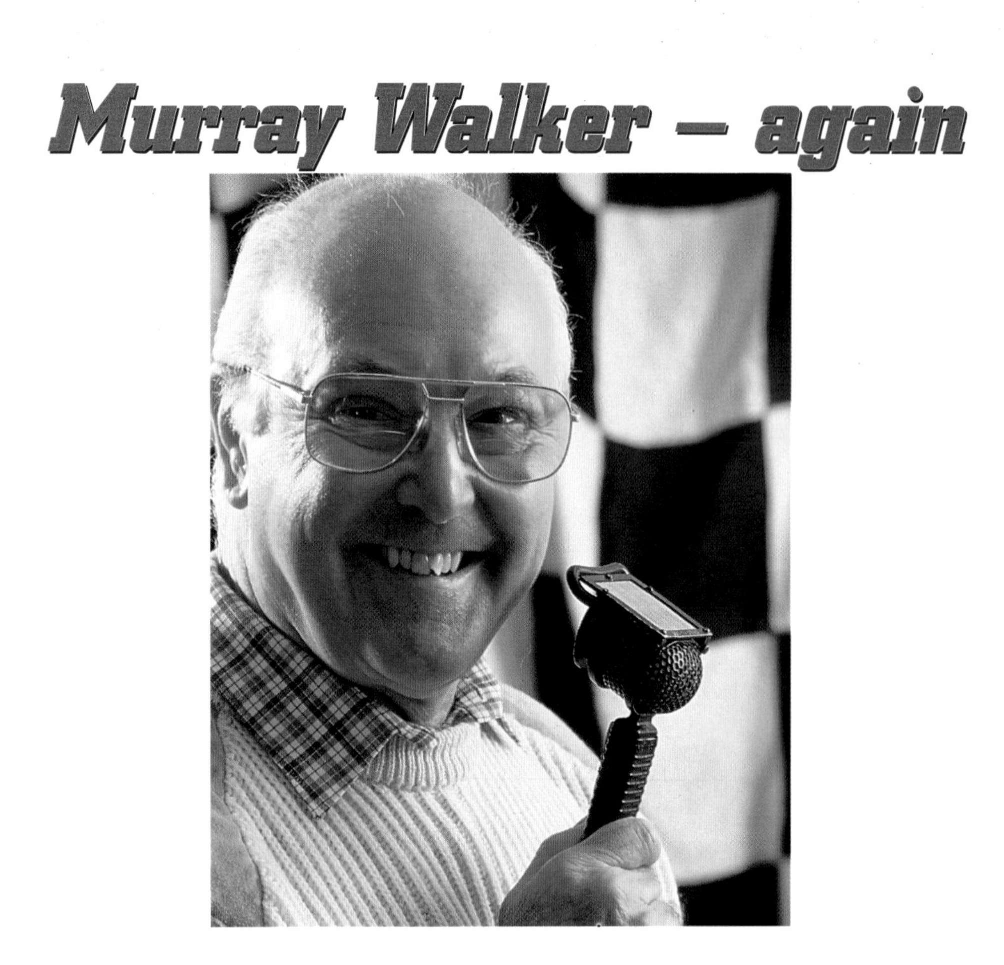

*"I make no apologies for their absence ...*
*I'm sorry they're not here."*

**– MURRAY WALKER**

*"If they have any shillelaghs in Suzuka, they'll be playing them tonight."*

*"Mansell is slowing down... he's taking it easy. Oh no he isn't! It's a lap record!"*

*"And now excuse me while I interrupt myself."*

*"The atmosphere is so tense that you could cut it with a cricket stump."*

*"He's obviously gone in for a wheel change and I say 'obviously' because I can't see."*

*"Nigel Mansell ... the Man of the Race ... the Man of the Day ...*
*the Man from the Isle of Man."*

*"Damon Hill is leading ... behind him are the second and third men."*

*"And Nelson Piquet must be furious with himself inside his helmet."*

*"Just under ten seconds for Nigel Mansell ...*
*call it nine point five seconds in round figures."*

# If you enjoyed this book, What about these!

All these books are available at your local book shop or can be ordered direct from the publisher.
Just list the titles you require and give your name address, including post code.
Prices and availability are subject to change without notice.

Please send to Chameleon Cash Sales, 106 Great Russell Street London WCIB 3LJ, a cheque or postal order for £7.99 and add the following for postage and packaging:

UK - £1.00 For the first book. 50p for the second and 30p for the third for each additional book up to a maximum of £3.00.
OVERSEAS -( including Eire ) £2.00 For the first book and £1.00 for the second and 50p for each additional book up to a maximum of £3.00.